OTTER NONSENSE

BY NORTON JUSTER

ILLUSTRATED BY MICHAEL WITTE

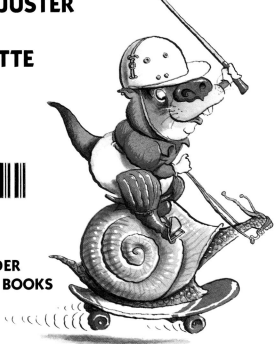

D0888146

BOOKS OF WONDER
MORROW JUNIOR BOOKS
New York

Pen and ink and watercolor were used for the full-color artwork.
The text type is 21-point Bernhard Modern.

Text copyright © 1982, 1994 by Norton Juster
Illustrations copyright © 1994 by Michael Witte

Printed in Singapore at Tien Wah Press.
1 2 3 4 5 6 7 8 9 10

Library of Congress Cataloging-in-Publication Data
Juster, Norton. Otter nonsense / by Norton Juster; illustrated by Michael Witte. p. cm. Summary: A
collection of puns based on animals, including "Fowl ball," "Crocoduel," and "Pupsicle."
ISBN 0-688-12282-5 (trade) — ISBN 0-688-12283-3 (library) 1. Animals—Juvenile humor.
2. Animals—Caricatures and cartoons—Juvenile literature. 3. Puns and punning.
[1. Animals—Wit and humor. 2. Puns and punning.] I. Witte, Michael C., ill. II. Title.
PN6231.A5J87 1994 818'.5402—dc20 93-22041 CIP AC

Patriotter

Seal of approval

Oxidentally
on
porpoise

An inchworm jumping
a foot out in the yard

Otter
control

Catastrophe

Pupsicle

Puppets

Soda
pup

Pupcorn

Pupulation explosion

Dog tired

A dandy lion lyin' down

Chipmonk

Wrendition

Wrendezvous

Apetite

Pig out

Bear up

Bear down

Baseball bats

Kangarookie

Striker otter

Fowl ball

Bunting

Ferret out

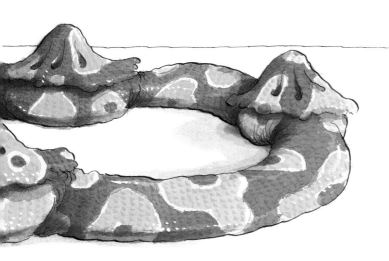

Piethon

Gopher broke

A hoarse horse horsing around in the horsepital

Larks and bagels

Otter space

Marsoupials

A froggy day

in London town

Fast buck

Terrible
cheetah

An aardvark and an even aarder vark taking a vark

A precarious perch

A sole survivor

with a
severe
haddock

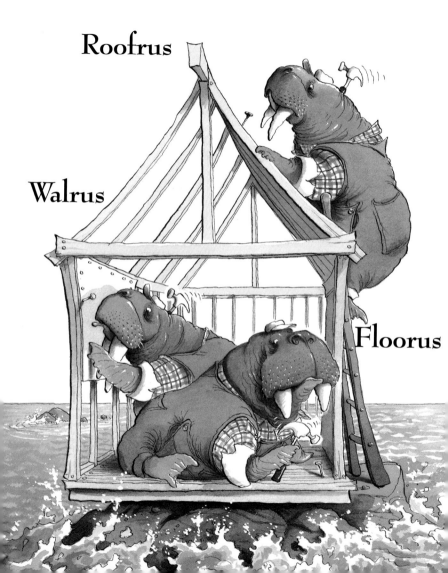

Plotter

Apeologize

Apelause

Wrenegade

Bisontennial

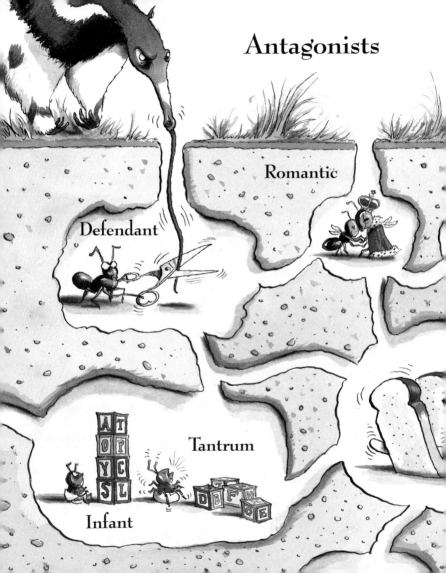

Crocodull

Crocoduel

Ostrich
and
poorcupine

Otter
the
blue

A moose with
a mousetache

A mouse with
a moosetache

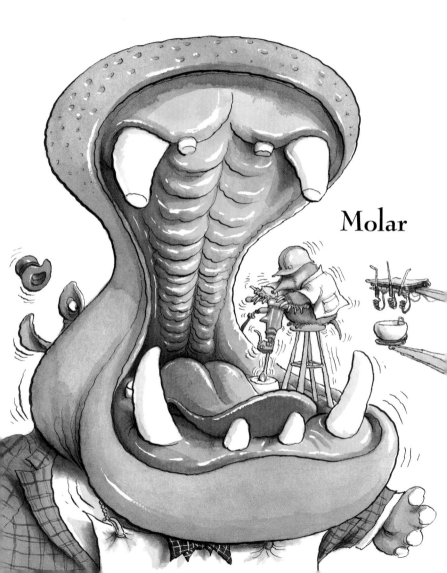

Molar

Hippopottymus

MARATHON

All the gnus that's fit to print

Heron gone

No newts is good newts

We hope you've had some fauna